TROPICAL
RAIN FORESTS

by Delia Goetz

Illustrated by Louis Darling

WILLIAM MORROW AND COMPANY
NEW YORK   1957

Tropical rain forests are places that are always hot, humid, and rainy. They are green the year round. Old leaves fall and new leaves appear at the same time, but the trees are never bare. It is never so dry or so cold that plants stop growing.

3

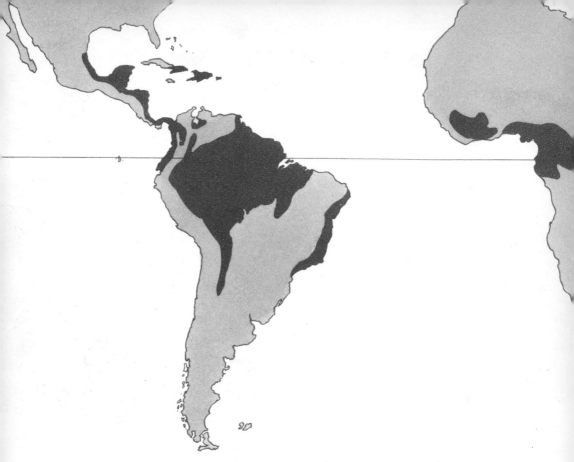

These rain forests make an irregular green belt around the earth near the equator. The belt is widest in the Amazon region of South America. In Africa it spreads over most of the Congo basin and includes patches along the Guinea coast. The rainy belt also covers parts of southeast Asia as well as a narrow border

4

along the western coast of India and Burma.

Smaller rain forests lie outside this belt. They edge Central America's east coast and cover parts of islands of the West Indies. They border western Colombia and Ecuador north of the equator, and sweep along Brazil's southeast coast.

Tropical rain forests are always hot and humid, because of their location and the amount of rainfall they receive. Since they lie near the equator, the sun's rays strike down almost directly at midday the year round. Days and nights are of equal length, with no great change in temperature.

Every day for most of the year, rain drenches the forest. The warm air rises just as it rises above a stove. Higher and higher it moves, carrying vapor with it. Far above the earth the air cools. The vapor condenses, and large clouds like white cotton form. The day grows hotter. More clouds form and become darker. The forest is silent, as if waiting.

Around midday the storm breaks. Thunder crashes. Flashes of lightning zigzag across the darkened sky. Strong winds sweep through the forest and sway the branches of mighty trees. Like pebbles dropping on a roof, raindrops pelt the thick leaves. Then comes the downpour. Rain falls on the forest as if a huge tank of water were overturned. Soon the shower is over, but the thunder continues to roll and grumble. The constant drip, drip, drip from the leaves sounds like a leaky faucet.

Then clouds begin to pile up again. They grow larger and larger, and darker and darker. The thunder is louder, lightning flashes, and again raindrops pelt the leaves. All afternoon storm after storm breaks over the forest. They end when evening comes and it is cooler.

No two tropical rain forests are just alike, yet they all look much the same. They all have dense vegetation and many different kinds of trees and plants; among a hundred trees growing together, only two or three may be alike. Nowhere else do trees and plants grow so fast. Plants shoot up overnight and grow quickly. Some, like the bamboo, may grow a foot a day. Some of the trees are a hundred and fifty feet tall. Their great crowns meet overhead, making a roof of green far above the forest floor.

Below, on the forest floor, the light is dim. Like a gigantic parasol, the great roof shuts out the sunlight. The air is warm and humid, like the air in a greenhouse. There is the smell of damp earth and plants, and the faint per-fume of flowers. Water drips from leaves and stands in pools and puddles. Fallen leaves and thick moss cover the ground. Within the forest there is silence.

Here, where the trees stand so close together, there are no low branches. But vines with woody stems like heavy cables grow upward on the trees. Some hug the tree trunk on which they climb. Others, after twisting their thick stems around a tree trunk, coil on the branches or hang in long loops. Some reach out and fasten themselves on other trees, weaving them together.

In the rain forests, plants grow upon plants. Some are parasites—plants that take their food from other plants. Unlike the parasites, air plants such as some orchids, mosses, and ferns make their home on other plants but take food and water from the air. They are roomers but not boarders.

Still other plants are stranglers. They begin to grow as air plants. Then branches shoot upward and close-growing roots drop downward to the earth. These roots finally merge into a rough, uneven trunk around the tree upon which they have grown. At last the tree dies.

These stranglers, as well as other forest trees, often have huge buttresses. These are growths which extend several feet at each side of the tree. The buttress is widest at the base of the tree, then tapers upward ten or more feet along the tree trunk.

STRANGLER FIG

Plants in the tropical rain forest have ways of getting along in the almost constant rain. Unlike desert plants, which must store water, these plants must get rid of it. Drip tips, the thin pointed tips of large leaves, act as spouts to carry water off the leaves.

Trees and plants may change their habits in the rain forest. Some palms develop tiny claws

BAMBOO, A GRASS

or hooks on the leaf, which hold them as they climb toward the light. Grasses may grow as high as a four-story house. Plants that are small in cool climates may become giants in the rain forest. Daisies are picked from rainforest trees. The periwinkle, which grows close to the ground in cool gardens, becomes a tree in the tropical rain forest.

15

MACAW

The world's largest tropical rain forest is in South America. For twenty-three hundred miles, from the eastern slopes of the Andes Mountains to the mouth of the Amazon River, it spreads a green roof over the earth. Like all tropical rain forests, it is warmed all year by the sun and drenched by rain almost daily. Light shining through chinks in the roof of leaves makes a dappled pattern on the forest floor. The forest is still and seems empty.

TOUCAN

Then an enormous butterfly drifts past on bright blue wings. A hummingbird lands lightly on a leaf. Thousands of parasol ants hurry past, each holding a bit of green leaf above its head. From the treetops comes the sound of harsh voices. Parrots and parakeets are feasting on fruits and nuts. A raucous-voiced macaw flies in to help itself. A brilliant toucan is there too, snapping its enormous bill.

17

Monkeys awakened from their naps scold and chatter. The widespread wings of a harpy eagle cast a dark shadow as it swoops down for a meal of bird, or monkey, or whatever it can find. Lower down in the forest, the booming voice of the giant tree frog is suddenly hushed as a long boa constrictor slides slowly onto a limb.

SQUIRREL MONKEY

JAGUAR

The rain forest, which at times is so still, is not empty. Only in the sea are there a greater number of living things. But like living things in the sea, those in the forest are seldom seen. Many live high in the treetops. Animals on the forest floor have ways of keeping out of sight. Jaguar and ocelot move silently through the forest. Only eyes trained to see in the forest notice the puma lying motionless on a branch. Snakes move as silently as thick oil flowing across the ground. Coiled on the trees, they look like the stout stems of vines.

19

Of all animals, none keeps itself better hidden than the sloth. Curled up for a nap in the fork of a tree, it looks like a huge ball of moss. No other animal is more of a sleepyhead. Once asleep, a sloth is almost impossible to waken. At last it begins to move. It touches a branch, then grasps it with its strong claws. Inch by inch it moves along until it is in its usual position, hanging upside down on a branch. Its blank little face looks up into the treetops. The sloth eats only one thing. For breakfast, dinner, supper, or snacks between, it feeds on the leaves of the cecropia tree.

TWO-TOED SLOTH

The sloth has none of the usual ways of protecting itself. It does not bite, never fights,
cannot run away. Jaguars, harpy eagles, and
other enemies try to snatch it from its branch.
But that is not easy to do. The sloth's muscles
are as strong as steel. Its claws stick to the
branch like burrs on a sweater. Under the fur
is skin as tough as leather.

Like the sloth, many other animals live in the trees. Most are seldom seen, but many of them are heard at some time of the day or night. Keen eyes may catch a glimpse of a wistful little face peering from the leaves. It belongs to a capuchin monkey, the organ-grinder's friend, and one of the most mis-chievous members of the entire monkey family. Soon he is up to his pranks, leaping, chattering, and tossing down sticks or fruit upon any living creature below. The screams of the red howler monkey are the most terri-fying sounds in the forest.

Some animals divide their time between treetops and ground. The coati, a close relative of the raccoon, lives in trees as well as on the forest floor. It climbs around in the trees as easily as a monkey and uses its long tail to balance itself. No tree is too high, no branch too long for a coati looking for something to eat. Eggs are its favorite food, but it will eat anything: bananas, berries, nuts, small birds, insects, and snakes.

The coati enjoys fighting almost as much as eating. It will tackle a puma or jaguar and never hesitates to tangle with another coati. Its keen smell and sight make it a hard animal to dodge.

COATI

TAPIR

Unlike the keen-eyed coati, the nearsighted tapir is an animal badly in need of spectacles. Some hunters say that it can see only about ten feet. It may run toward a man as if to attack, but it does not know he is there. The tapir is shy, gentle, and not at all dangerous. It eats all kinds of plants.

When men or animals hear a clicking, snapping sound in the rain forest, men climb trees

PECCARY

and animals try to run away. They know that
peccaries (wild pigs) are coming. No other
forest animal is more feared than the white-
lipped peccary. It is small and spindle-legged,
but those spindly legs travel fast to capture
prey or to escape from an enemy. The peccary
has tusks as sharp as razors in both jaws. With
them, it makes quick work of whatever comes
its way.

Few of the animals in the Amazon rain forest will attack a man. But worse than dangerous beasts or poisonous snakes are the millions of insects that make life miserable. They are everywhere. There is no escaping them. The tiny red ant's bite is like a flame over the body, but it leaves few ill effects. Buzzing mosquitoes annoy and sting, and some cause malaria.

The person who goes barefoot may find that chigoes have laid eggs in the soles of his feet. These tiny insects burrow under the skin and lay dozens of eggs, enclosed in a little sac. If they are not taken out in time, it may mean the loss of a toe or two.

TSETSE FLY

Most destructive of all are the army ants. Some move in single file and others march three or four abreast to tackle a job, like a well-trained army. Wherever they go, they destroy everything. Animals, insects, birds, snakes — everything in the forest tries to escape them. Within a short time they can strip the flesh from a large animal. A wounded and helpless man in their path never escapes them.

In the rain forests of Africa and Asia, insects also make man's life miserable. Africa's tsetse fly is one of the worst. It attacks man and beast. Only recently has a cure been found for the sleeping sickness caused by its bite.

27

African and Asian rain forests have many birds and animals identical or similar to those living in American forests. Countless members of the brightly colored parrot family flash through the treetops. Golden-colored sunbirds resemble the hummingbird of America but do not belong to the same family.

The hornbill that lives high in the treetops of the Old World forests has the enormous bill and gaudy colors of the South American toucan. The hornbill, however, has a peculiar habit which the toucan does not share. When his mate lays her eggs in a nest in a hollow tree, the male hornbill seals her in with a wall of mud. In the wall he leaves an opening just large enough to push food through. There she stays until the young birds are ready to fly. Then the father hornbill opens the wall and the whole family takes off on a noisy flight.

HORNBILL

Many relatives of the monkeys and apes that live in American forests leap through the branches in Africa and Asia. In the dense forests of Malaya the large orangutan walks upright and may be as tall as three feet or more. Its face and reddish color resemble those of the Amazon's red howler monkey.

ORANGUTAN

GIANT ANTEATER

The tapir of Malaya is similar in looks and habits to its shy, nearsighted relative in the Amazon forest. Anteaters, wherever they live, are as odd-looking as those in the Americas. Tigers, leopards, and panthers move noiselessly through African and Asian forests. Most of them lurk at the edge of the rain forest and near watering places.

The rain forests of Asia and Africa have some animals that are not found in the forests of America. Elephants live both in Africa and Asia, but they differ in size and disposition. The African elephant is larger, and hunting him is a dangerous sport. The smaller Asian elephant has a better disposition and is more easily trained.

INDIAN
ELEPHANT

AFRICAN
ELEPHANT

RHINOCEROS

The rhinoceros is another animal of the African and Asian rain forests that does not live in America. It is often called the rain-forest grouch, for no other animal wears a more surly expression or looks so untidy. Its skin hangs in folds and wrinkles, as if it belonged to its big brother. Ticks infest the folds of the rhino's ill-fitting skin. They provide meals for the tickbird that spends so much time on the broad back of the rhinoceros. The bird's shrill cries are said to warn its host of hunters or other enemies. So both bird and beast benefit from the arrangement.

OKAPI

Each rain forest also has wild life which lives in no other place. An example is the okapi, a shy animal that lives only in the dense part of the African forest. It is about the size of a horse and has a purplish body, cream-colored legs ringed with black like a zebra's, and a long slender neck and small head resembling those of a giraffe.

In rain forests around the world there are bats and rats, squirrels that fly, and animals that carry their young in pouches. Dangerous snakes live in all rain forests—among them, anacondas, cobras, and bushmasters.

BOA CONSTRICTOR

Tropical rain forests may not seem like pleasant places to live in, but people make their homes in some parts of all of them. Some of these people are seen as seldom as the animals and birds that live in the treetops. As silently as the jaguar or puma, they move through the forests. In the forests of Africa, America, or Asia, people live in much the same way. From the forest they get their houses, their food, and the few clothes they wear. Yet these people present many contrasts—in their looks and their lives, in the languages they speak and the customs they follow.

Many different Indian tribes live in the Amazon rain forest. Some are savages who kill their enemies with spears and darts tipped with poison. Some are head-hunters who shrink the heads of their victims. But more of them are people who live in peace with men of other tribes and races.

Some forest dwellers are hunters, who bring down their game with bows and arrows or long blowguns. From the streams they get fish; from the forest they gather berries, nuts, and fruit. These are the nomads of the forest, moving from one campfire to another. They build no home except rude shelters of branches

and leaves. They do not farm or work for others. The Negritos, or pygmies, living deep within the forests of Asia and Africa, are examples of such hunters. White men seldom catch more than a glimpse of these tiny brown-skinned, tousled-haired men, for they are as shy as the most timid animals.

Indians of the Amazon live in clearings in the forest or along the banks of rivers. In some villages all the people live in one large building. In others each family has a house of its own. Whether the house is large or small, it is made of trees from the forest. The roof is a thatch of leaves, and the walls are often made of green branches covered with mud, or are woven of leaves. A few straw mats are the only furnishings. A hammock woven of fibers drawn from plants is the bed. Tools, clothes, boats, and dishes are made from materials the Indians find around them.

When the land is cleared, fields and gardens are planted. The main crop is the cassava, or manioc. The root is ground to make a kind of flour. With this flour is made the thin, crisp pancake that is the bread of the Amazon rainforest people. Beans, corn, bananas, and yams

MAKING CASSAVA BREAD

grow quickly in the damp soil and hot climate.

Even if carefully tended, a crop may disappear before harvest. Ants may strip the fields in one night. A tapir may make a feast of the vegetables. A cloudburst may wash the new fields away, but another crop soon grows.

Forest people also find food in streams and rivers. Turtles make a good meal. So do the eggs which they lay in the warm sands. But danger lurks in the waters that supply food. Alligators and crocodiles are hard to tell from a log in the water. An anaconda, the huge serpent that lives along the rivers and in the forests of the Amazon, may attack a fisherman. But it is the piranha, a bloodthirsty fish, that the fisherman fears most. A few drops of blood on the water bring it racing from the bottom of the river. No matter how big the wounded man or beast, the piranha's sharp teeth leave only the skeleton.

PIRANHA

Fish are always to be had from the rivers, but cleared land will produce crops for only a few years. The hot sun burns the soil and the rain washes needed minerals away. Then it is time to move on and make a new clearing. Moving day means little work for the people of the rain forest. They take down hammocks, roll up mats, pick up pans and manioc grater, and move on. Quickly the clearing is over-grown with vines and grasses and small trees, and becomes a tangled jungle.

Negroes of the African rain forests clear land and make farms in much the same way as the Indians of the Amazon. Most of them also have pigs, some poultry, a few goats, and a dog or two.

The rain forests of Asia have been compared to a huge mixing bowl into which people of many races and colors have been poured. They are black, brown, yellow, white, and all the shades between. Some people are short; others are tall. Each group has its own language, customs, and beliefs.

Back from the cities, deep in the forests, these people live in much the same way as the forest dwellers of Africa and the Americas. A village storyteller takes the place of radio and TV. There are special days to celebrate with music and dancing and feasts. Artists mold clay into bowls of pleasing shapes, carve figures from wood and ivory, or make tools that are both practical and beautiful.

BALINESE DANCER

Children do not go to schools such as we know. Yet every child of the forest has lessons to learn. He learns which plants are good to eat and which cure the sick. Here is the plant that stuns fish and makes them easy to catch. There is the plant that yields poison

with which to tip the dart or spear of the
hunter. He learns to know the footprints of
the leopard and the trail made by the anaconda as its heavy body slides over soft ground.
He must memorize the rituals to follow and
learn the signs that foretell good fortune or
bad.

Unlike the sparsely settled rain forests of America and Africa, those of Asia have many inhabitants. These people furnish the labor needed to bring products from the forests and to work the plantations. For these tropical rain forests are rich storehouses of valuable products on which most of us depend every day.

Spices in our cupboards; medicines in drugstores; oil for salads, machinery, or toilet creams; chocolate and chewing gum and nuts; erasers and rubber tires; furniture and boats; balsa wood for model airplanes and rafts — these are only a few of the products for which we depend on the rain forests.

The coconut palm furnishes so many of man's needs that it is often called the tree of a hundred uses. Its fruit is good to eat and its milk is a refreshing drink. The bud is used as a vegetable. Fibers drawn from the husk of the coconut are twisted into rope, woven into mats and cloth, or used to make brushes. Houses and boats are built from the tree trunk, and branches make fuel for the fire. Copra, the dried meat of the coconut, is a rich source of oil which is used in making candy, margarine, candles, shampoos, and many other products.

To the people of Africa, the oil palm is as important as the coconut palm is in parts of the Americas and Asia.

The people who collected nuts and cacao and tapped rubber trees in the forest could not keep up with the demand for these products. Far from the rain forests, more and more people wanted tires and oils and spices and other products dependent upon plants growing there. Great plantations were developed for growing rubber trees and oil palms and cacao. Trees and plants grown on carefully tended plantations yielded more than those growing wild. It was easier to collect these materials on plantations than to search for them in the forests. More and more of the rain forests in Africa and America are being cleared for plantations. Highways and railroads have been built to bring out the products.

Life is changing, too, for some of the people who collect forest products and carry them to market. In schools at the edge of the forest they are learning new lessons. They are laying down their handmade hoes and axes to drive tractors and jeeps. They are putting aside tribal dress to wear the white man's clothes. Telephones carry messages once sent by drums.

Modern cities stand at the edge of the rain forests. Air conditioning makes life more comfortable for some of the people working there. New drugs are helping to keep them healthy. Soon, some men say, many more people will live in all of the rain forests, and all forest products will be grown on plantations.

Others disagree. Tropical rain forests, they say, will never be healthful places to live in. Clearing the forests, they warn, will ruin the land.

Scientists say that we have only begun to know and use the tropical rain forests. They point out that only there can much of the world's plant and animal life be studied.

Day after day, high on platforms built in the forests, these men sit with cameras and notebooks. The information they gather may help to find new foods or medicines, or other valuable products. Many people believe that we must take steps to protect these great treasure houses—our tropical rain forests.